THE VETERAN'S LONG TERM CARE SOLUTION

The Truth Behind Long Term Care Planning for Veterans with the Aid and Attendance Pension Benefit Explained in Plain English

Jeffrey G. Marsocci, Esq.
Certified Medicaid Planner™
Accredited V.A. Attorney

Domestic Partner Publishing, LLC

Note Regarding Information

As with any product, it is important to be clear about its intended purpose and use to avoid any misunderstandings. Specifically with writings about legal issues, it is noted that these materials are not a substitute for competent legal counsel. The contents of this guide are instead written to provide information about common estate planning problems faced by domestic partners, and it is designed for general educational purposes only. The contents of this guide are not to be construed as legal advice, and no attorney-client privilege exists between the reader and the author and/or publisher. In addition, laws change frequently, and therefore you also are urged to speak with an attorney about changes in the law that may affect you.

Circular 230 Disclosure: To ensure compliance with requirements imposed by the Internal Revenue Service, unless specifically indicated otherwise, any tax advice contained in this communication (including any accompanying literature) was not intended or written to be used, and cannot be used, for the purpose of avoiding tax-related penalties or promoting, marketing, or recommending to another party any tax-related matter addressed herein. For specific legal advice, you are urged to contact an attorney in your state or jurisdiction.

About the Author

Jeffrey G. Marsocci was born in Fort Worth, Texas, and raised in Lincoln, Rhode Island, where he graduated from Mount Saint Charles Academy High School. He received his Bachelor's degree in Business from Hofstra University, and two years later earned his law degree from the same university.

In 2004, he received a Certificate Degree in Non-Profit Management from Duke University. Jeff also served as a member of the Legal Council for The Estate Planning Source, LLC, a nationally recognized estate preservation company formed by the protégés of the late Henry W. Abts III, trust guru and author of The Living Trust. In 2012, Mr. Marsocci was admitted as V.A. Accredited Attorney for the preparation, presentation, and prosecution of claims before the Department of Veterans Affairs in order to focus on assisting clients qualify for the Aid and Attendance Pension Benefit. In 2014, he was credentialed as a Certified Medicaid Planner™ by the CMP Governing Board for meeting education and experience requirements, showing proficiency in Medicaid Planning through a thorough examination, and committing to adhere to the highest in professional standards.

Mr. Marsocci has led his own firm in Raleigh, North Carolina, since 1996, focusing on the areas of V.A. Pension Benefit asset protection, Medicaid Planning, and general Trusts and Estate Planning. He also frequently participates in national and regional programs to educate attorneys, financial advisors and accountants on estate planning issues.

Jeff and his wife Kathleen work with the college-based service organization Circle K at North Carolina State University. Jeff and Kathy also each received the President's Call to Service Award for performing more than 4,000 hours of service during their lifetimes.

This book is dedicated to those who served.

Special Thanks to
David Cole and The Senior Veterans Council
for their contributions to this book
without whose help the book wouldn't be possible.

TABLE OF CONTENTS

Foreword		1
Introduction		5
Chapter One	Ten Myths of Care Assistance Planning for Veterans	13
Chapter Two	Your Basic Care Options	21
Chapter Three	Ways to Pay for Long Term Care	27
Chapter Four	The Service Qualification Test	35
Chapter Five	The Income Test	41
Chapter Six	The Asset Test	47
Chapter Seven	Comprehensive Solutions	53
Chapter Eight	Finding the Right Professionals	65
Chapter Nine	Financial and Investment Options	75
Chapter Ten	Some Medicaid Qualification Rules	85
Chapter Eleven	Avoiding Bad Advice	97
Afternote		107

Foreword

When Jeff mentioned that he was writing a book about the intricacies of what the V.A. itself calls "the least known and most underutilized benefit the V.A. offers," I was eager to help in any way I could. For several years Jeff and I have worked with clients to help Senior War-Time Veterans and their widows gain access to benefits they earned by service to their country during a period of war. Because this benefit has been around since the end of the civil war, it has, unfortunately, become layered in a bureaucratic maze that most are unable to navigate successfully without professional help. At least, not quickly, the first time.

As accredited V.A. Claims agents, Senior Veterans Council works primarily with World War II, Korean and Vietnam Veterans who have reached that stage in their life where they need what the V.A. calls "some assistance with some activities of ordinary daily living," meaning those things that most of us take for granted, such as bathing, dressing, and a few other things. The premise of this little known benefit is that because the Veteran (or his widow) was there when we needed them, the country will help now that they need help.

One of the main reasons I am in this business is because I have seen this work change lives. Not just with the award of a monthly cash benefit from the V.A., but with the support our respective offices to provide with "end of life, worst-case planning for care needs." In addition to the legal planning and framework that Jeff and his office provides, our office has developed a team of long-term care planning and resource specialists, such as a Registered Nurse, a Geriatric Care Manager, and a Social Worker to help our clients understand not just the V.A. Benefit, but a number of other government, social, and community benefits that may be available.

This work assures that Veterans and their widows receive not only the benefits they earned by their service, but also other benefits they earned by the hundreds of thousands in taxes they paid over their lifetime. Our files our filled with letters from clients and their families telling us how the benefits changed their lives, which, for me, makes the hard work all worthwhile.

What can you expect from reading this book? – First Jeff's "hold no punches" style is honest, refreshing, and easy to understand that lays out in clear language what you'll face when working with the V.A.. It is definitely not a legal tome of information written in that foreign language we call "legalese."

Next, by taking the time to read this book, you'll better understand how to access a range of V.A. Benefits by avoiding the many land mines that get in the way of most claims. There certainly are a lot of rumors, folk tales, and misconceptions out there about what it actually takes to qualify for certain benefits, and this book exposes some of the bigger ones.

Third, the challenges of providing end of life planning for care needs are rarely easy, and this book does go over some of those decisions. Once a senior family member reaches the time when they need help with the things that the rest of us take for granted, things never get better, they only get worse, with death being the final release from those challenges. But if preparations are not made, end of life issues will create even more problems.

These topics are sometimes unpleasant to contemplate, but they must be addressed, and the sooner they are addressed, the better. Putting the discussion off only deepens the problems ahead. More importantly, putting things off can mean that a Veteran or their widow is losing out on financial help they are entitled to.

The good news is that Jeff is one of the most focused, dedicated attorneys that I have worked with over the years. And that says a lot because I've work with a lot of attorneys in just about all 50 states. So kick back, find a quiet spot, dig into this short read, and enjoy Jeff's stories and insights that can truly change your life.

Introduction

Thank you for reading this book on long term care for Veterans. Families face many challenges as their loved ones age, and the costs of long term care can be one of the most daunting. Thousands and thousands of dollars may be spent, income alone may not be enough to pay bills, and then a lifetime of building assets can be drained trying to pay for care. But there is help, particularly for those who served their country during war time. But the government does not make it easy, and in particular the Aid and Attendance Pension Benefit (often mislabeled as the "Aid and Attendance benefit") is one of the most hidden programs available. I've been working in the field of long term care planning as an attorney for more than 23 years now, and I can tell you the one thing that the government does NOT want you to know... that you do not have to go broke and lose everything to qualify for the various government Care Assistance programs that you spent a lifetime paying into through taxes, and especially those you have earned serving your country.

As an experienced planning professional, V.A. Accredited Attorney, and a Certified Medicaid Planner™, I am happy to help you learn the basics of Care Assistance Planning for veterans, their spouses, and their widows and widowers BEFORE you begin rearranging assets. One thing I can tell you about long term care assistance qualification is that it is never simple and it is never a matter of taking the same three steps that everyone else does.

Each situation is unique, and getting one little thing wrong can cause the entire plan to implode.

However, something else I have learned is that knowing the rules around the Aid and Attendance Pension Benefit can lead to proper planning, creative solutions, and often can help with possible Medicaid long term care assistance qualification down the road. In fact, there are many similarities in the comprehensive "toolbox" plan we use for the Veterans Benefit that are also included in a Medicaid Plan. And in the case of the Aid and Attendance Pension Benefit, the sooner you get started, the sooner the pension from the V.A. can begin to help you pay for the help you need. But before we begin, I want to address something.

I know you have a lot of questions, and it is extremely important to ask these questions before taking action.

- How do people shelter a lifetime worth of assets when the Department of Veterans Affairs, and other government offices, seem to want people to be broke?

- Do people simply give everything away?

- Isn't it true that planning has to be done five years before the Aid and Attendance Benefit is ever needed?

- (For the kids) Is there anything I can do if Mom or Dad has to go into an assisted living facility or nursing home in the next few weeks?

- How do I find professionals who actually know their stuff?

I'm going to cover all of this and many other useful bits of information. As the qualification for the Aid and Attendance Pension Benefit and Medicaid are the Care Assistance topics veterans and their families generally want answers to very quickly, I have divided the chapters into simple parts with the initial materials focused on the Aid and Attendance Pension Benefit and then towards the back of the book the information will be more focused on Medicaid solutions. Why? How does Medicaid qualification affect veterans, their spouse, or their widow or widower? The reason we are addressing both programs is because *the solutions* surrounding both programs are similar, despite some of the rules for qualification being vastly different. But please do not think that the money is all Care Assistance is about. For example, did you know there are four basic ways to pay for long term health care? There is long term care insurance. However, many people consider it to be too expensive by the time they need it. Then there is a properly constructed and explained Care Assistance Plan unique to each situation. But there are third and fourth options. Most people choose one of them and it's deadly to long term planning.

There are specialized trusts that can help with Care Assistance Planning for both the Aid and Attendance Benefit and Medicaid, but timing is everything, not all trusts are the same, and trusts may only be a small part of a comprehensive plan. But as I said before, having the right toolbox of trusts and other documents can greatly help attain the when the need for nursing level care arises.

But it is not just about the documents. It is also about the professionals working with you. Did you know there are four things to look for when seeking Aid and Attendance Pension Benefit professionals or attorneys before you hire them? This one qualification and three questions show you without a shadow of a doubt if they have the background and knowledge to help you with your plans. Hire the wrong person and you and your family could run into problems.

These are just a few of the tips I'll provide in this book. Here's what we'll cover:

Chapter One: *Ten Myths of Care Assistance Planning for Veterans.* Nearly everyone I have spoken to believes one or more of these myths about Aid and Attendance Pension Benefit or Medicaid Planning are absolutely true, and it can put your home and your life savings at risk.

Chapter Two: *Your Basic Care Options.* There are four basic care options when it comes to long term care planning. In many cases, people will go through more than one type of care during life, but it is important to know the different options as well as the pros and cons of each.

Chapter Three: *Ways to Pay for Long Term Care.* There are four main ways to pay for long term care, and the right kind of financial and legal planning well in advance can make all of the difference in the world. But even in cases when there is not a lot of time, specifically for Veterans needing care, you can often preserve substantial assets for your loved ones.

Chapter Four: *The Service Qualification Test.* There are several specific tests surrounding a veteran's service that needs to be examined. While the rules are stated simply, there is a lot of misconceptions around whether a person qualifies for the benefit, and many more people qualify for the Aid and Attendance Pension Benefit when they originally believed they didn't.

Chapter Five: *The Income Test*, and how the Department of Veterans Affairs looks at income for individuals and married couples. While the income rules for the Aid and Attendance Pension Benefit are complex, there is actually a simple framework in viewing how your income affects qualification.

Chapter Six: *The Asset Test* as used in Aid and Attendance Pension Benefit planning, and how these rules are applied. How your assets are looked at for qualification, and while it appears you have to be broke or nearly broke to qualify for the Aid and Attendance Pension Benefit (again commonly misnamed the Aid and Attendance Veterans Benefit), there are many ways to maximize assets and minimize a spend-down for you and your family.

Chapter Seven: *Comprehensive Solutions.* With enough lead time before custodial care is actually needed, there is a single box of legal and financial tools that will provide a good overall Care Assistance professional many, many options in protecting assets for the family as possible, but not all of the tools are necessarily needed for qualification for the Aid and Attendance Pension Benefit. While it may turn out that only a few of the tools will actually be needed, it is best to have all of these tools *for the particular program we are looking at* and not come up short later if the situation changes.

Chapter Eight: *Finding the Right Professionals.* The three questions and one credential that can help you find the right professionals to help with the Aid and Attendance Pension Benefit. Because Medicaid planning is always a factor to be reviewed in conjunction with setting up a plan to qualify for the pension, and because there are more than 200,000 rules for Medicaid-based Care Assistance alone and everyone's assets are different, this lesson comes with a big disclaimer that this is not a guideline to creating your own plan. In fact, it is our personal guarantee that simply copying what others have done will lead to you being disqualified for Medicaid assistance down the road, not qualifying for the Aid and Attendance Pension Benefit, or simply wasting a lot of money.

Chapter Nine: *Financial and Investment Options.* Once assets have been transferred in accordance with the plan, we are often left with a child of the veteran or their spouse/widowe(er) acting as trustee of an irrevocable trust. How should those assets be protected from loss, make some gains, and yet properly balance the possible need for assets to remain liquid in case they are needed to pay for care or other items? In this chapter, we'll examine some of the most common factors and investment solutions we see.

Chapter Ten: *Some Medicaid Qualification Rules.* While the primary aim for this book is to provide education around the Aid and Attendance Pension Benefit, Medicaid should always be a factor in creating a good Care Assistance Plan.

Chapter Eleven: *Avoiding Bad Advice.* Too many times, well meaning (and not so well meaning) professionals interfere in the overall plan, focusing on what they know in their small puzzle piece without looking at the whole puzzle.

While all of these chapters provide good information, each is only a small part of the vast puzzle that is the legal end of qualifying for the Aid and Attendance Pension Benefit. In fact, these chapters only scratch the surface of overall Care Assistance Planning. For legal and regulatory reasons, we have to provide a disclaimer that all of these materials are not legal advice, but here are two pieces of actual, direct advice that I will unequivocally stand behind:

1) DON'T TAKE PIECEMEAL ACTIONS ON YOUR OWN BECAUSE IT CAN CAUSE AN UNCHANGEABLE DISASTER; and

2) GET HELP FROM THE RIGHT PROFESSIONALS.

Hopefully this information will prove useful to you, but in the meantime take notes. Working with a good team of professionals can make all of the difference, and you should line up any important questions you may have before you meet with them. If you have questions, then please call my office at 919-844-7993.

Chapter One:
Ten Myths of Care Assistance Planning for Veterans

"Well, I don't know," she said. "I don't think we would qualify."

"I think you would," I said. "He needs the help, and you can't just keep doing it yourself. He's a big guy whose dementia is worsening. You need to hire someone to help out. Otherwise, it will just keep wearing you down. Eventually, you won't be able to keep up."

"But I'm happy to do it," she said. "He's my husband, and it really isn't that tough."

"That's not what I've been hearing from your niece," I said, being honest. "She tells me you're taking on too much, and you need some time for yourself and to rest."

"Well, anyway, I don't think it matters," she said. "I know we have too much income and we have too much in savings to qualify for the benefit you were telling me about."

"Again, I do think you'll qualify," I said. "Just call him, fill out the paperwork, and do what he says. The Senior Veterans Council has been doing this for years, and they know their stuff. He was there to serve his country when they needed him in Korea, and he is now entitled to this help from his country when he needs it."

I specifically didn't use any names in this story because it is based on the story of some of my own family members. But she did call, she did look into things, she did provide the needed paperwork, and then suddenly there was money each month to help pay for a home health aide to come in three times a week. This made sure that she was able to go out with her friends, visit with relatives, or just get some extra sleep when she needed it.

Unfortunately, he did pass on several years after qualifying for the Aid and Attendance Pension Benefit, dying at home surrounded by his family, and with the proper medical help and care he needed. But just as important was having that help probably means that she will be with us for many more years. I've seen far too many caregivers go before their loved ones because they wear themselves out. And just as unfortunately this happens to too many people because they believe the myths and misconceptions that are out there.

There are a lot of myths surrounding the Care Assistance process, particularly when it comes to the Veterans and the Aid and Attendance Pension Benefit since the program is practically "hidden" from the general public. There is very little publicity around this assistance program, and because of that many times the information is not always accurate. Unfortunately, the consequences of incorrect information are often very costly to senior veterans who need it the most. That is why I have compiled the Top Ten Myths of Care Assistance Planning for Veterans. If you believe even one of these is true, failing to get the right information and may mean missing out on thousands of dollars of each month.

10 Myths That Can Put Your Home and Savings at Risk

Myth 10. *You have too much income to qualify for the Aid and Attendance Pension Benefit.* I hear from far too many veterans that they heard about the Aid and Attendance Pension Benefit (or, more likely, they heard about it as the "Aid and Attendance" benefit), and they decided to call the Veterans Administration about it. The conversations usually go something like this:

V.A. Staff Person: "How much do you (or you and your spouse) have each year."

Veteran: "We make $X per year."

V.A. Staff Person: "Oh, I'm sorry. Your income is too high to qualify."

Veteran: "OK. Thanks for checking for me."

Unfortunately, the veteran and their family members believe that is the end of it. But often it is not. And not looking a little further can cost you tens of thousands of dollars a year.

Myth 9. *You have too many assets to qualify for the Aid and Attendance Pension Benefit.* Often, this one is true to begin with, but there are ways to reposition and yet protect assets to easily qualify for the Aid and Attendance Pension Benefit. With the right documents and the right professional help, the asset test is often easily passed.

Myth 8. *The V.A. automatically takes care of veterans who need assisted living*. While it is true there are many programs available to help disabled veterans or veterans needing *nursing* level care (but with varying degrees of success and efficiency), there is no automatic coverage for *assisted living* levels of care.

Myth 7. *If you need help, just call the V.A.*. While the Veterans Administration is supposed to be there to help you, and the workers at the V.A. are often great people who want to help you, they are hamstringed by rules and procedures. There are often things they *want* to say to you but *can't*. When it comes to the Aid and Attendance Pension Benefit, the V.A. is limited to running quick numbers and processing applications. They are not allowed to tell you that you may transfer assets, engage family home health aides, or anything else that may help you qualify. This is because the advice they may want to give would technically be practicing law or if misunderstood by the veteran or their family could lead to disastrous consequences that could be blamed on the V.A. employee.

Myth 6. *You can qualify for the Veterans Pension by just giving your assets away*. Unfortunately, this one is just true enough to be truly dangerous. It's the one step planning that could be a step off a cliff. What if you give all of your assets to your son, and he ends up in a divorce or sued? Or what if he ends up in a divorce? Will all of your assets your son was "holding" for you be put at risk? Possibly. Or what if your son dies before you do? Will his spouse or kids honor the fact that it is your money that is supposed to be there for you if you need it? There are much better planning alternatives.

Myth 5. *Assets in my revocable living trust don't count towards a Aid and Attendance Pension Benefit spend down*. While revocable living trusts are excellent estate planning tools and, in certain circumstances, can assist with a *Medicaid* spend down for married couples, it does not simply exempt assets from the V.A.'s scrutiny.

Myth 4. *I'm sure I can just fill in the forms with the V.A. myself, so there's no need to have professionals help.* Again, this one has just enough truth in it to be dangerous. Because it is not all about just filling out an application. In fact, Veterans Claims Agents will assist with simply filling out forms by providing the correct forms and guidance in the process for free. But there are a whole host of other factors that extend far beyond the actual Aid and Attendance Pension Benefit application, including the arrangement of supporting documentation, assistance with the transfer of assets, developing the right trusts and care contracts, and looking down the road for the potential need of Medicaid and how those transfers would affect it. Like drafting your own trust documents, this is something veterans and their families just want to make sure they get right. Unfortunately we regularly receive calls from "do-it-yourself families" who were not only denied the benefit because the application was not submitted correctly, but they also were precluded from applying again for one year.

Myth 3. *If the V.A. won't pay for assisted living care, then I'm sure Medicare pays for all medical conditions, even ones lasting longer than 100 days*. The fact is that Medicare is a type of primary health insurance for seniors that takes care of a limited amount of services for a limited period of time. It does not pay for all long term care needs. Not nursing level care, and not even for hospital care beyond the stipulated number of days.

Myth 2. *My Medicare Supplement or Long Term Care Policy should just take care of assisted living or home health care*. Medicare supplements are designed to pick up the costs of co-pays and deductibles which are required for hospital care, not assisted living. And long term care insurance is *often* only covering nursing level care. I say "often" because there are some very good (and expensive) long term care insurance policies out there that will pay for some home health care services that are not considered "nursing" level, but even many of long term care policies that do cover home health care are focused on the nursing level of care. Meaning they are great for providing money to get you the same care as a nursing home in your own home or that of a child or other relative. But they often won't help with assisted living levels of care like the Aid and Attendance Pension Benefit is renowned for.

Myth 1. *There's no need for a comprehensive Aid and Attendance Pension Benefit Plan... my friend/neighbor/barista just did "X" and everything turned out OK*. The rules around qualification for the Aid and Attendance Pension Benefit are vast with many stipulations and exceptions. There are also more than 200,000 regulations surrounding the Medicaid portion of Care Assistance Planning (let alone other Care Assistance programs) that may be affected down the road by transfers or care arrangements that are improperly made. Finally, there are just as many combinations of strategies and techniques that can be used to benefit you, all depending on you and your family's unique situation. It is a huge mistake to think that everything will be clear because you *think* you understand 3 pieces of a 200,000 piece puzzle. It's always best to discuss things with Care Assistance professionals before taking action. What turned out well for your friend or neighbor may end up being a disaster for you.

With any luck, you have recognized some of these items as myths to begin with, but don't feel bad if you didn't. The Aid and Attendance Pension Benefit and qualifying for it is an extremely complicated area with an astounding number of traps and loopholes, and unless you make a career out of it you are not likely to know these myths from general reading and information from non-professionals. The main point I want to leave you with in this section is that Aid and Attendance Pension Benefit planning is far from simple. There can be a lot of savings and income to help with care costs for the family if planning is done correctly… and huge potential financial losses if done incorrectly.

Chapter Two:
Your Basic Care Options

It's times like this that I really understood why it's important to have a support staff and colleagues for planning around the Aid and Attendance Pension Benefit. While Jack (not his real name) was well organized, he knew he was in over his head and sought help. While Alyssa helped him organize some papers, Kathy brought him a glass of water and he was starting to look a little more at ease. Then he started in, talking faster than one of those disclaimers for a prescription drug you hear on the radio.

"Look, Jeff," Jack said. "I know that my dad's going to need help, and it's going to cost money. But he is a Vietnam veteran, and I know there has to be some help for him from the V.A. I just don't know how much, and I need to make sure that his assets are going to last. I know there's some shifting around we can do with her accounts, but there seems to be so much conflicting stuff out there. What should we do?"

"Slow down for a moment," I said, holding my hand up and talking deliberately slower. "Before we go into any of that, how is your dad doing?"

Jack looked a little taken aback. "I… didn't really expect you to ask that," he said, smiling. "Other people I have spoken to didn't seem to know what they were talking about, but all they wanted to talk about were his assets and income."

I smiled. "It's a good thing you came here then," I replied. "Before we can do anything about your father's *assets,* *we need to make sure we know what kind of* *care* *he needs. While I want to know what the medical professionals think, I first want to know how you think your dad is doing and what kind of help you think he needs. Is he in good spirits?"*

Planning around the Aid and Attendance Pension Benefit has to be about more than assets, income, and medical reports. Unfortunately, many professionals push those other items aside and focus only on the money. That is one reason why my office works with The Senior Veterans Council who has a geriatric care manager, social worker, and registered nurse, and other professionals on staff to provide evaluation advice and a care plan, and, to the extent our clients allow, we involve the family as well. After all, the decision on a parent's long term personal care often involves the family as much as the veteran, spouse, or widow's parent.

The different options available relate often to what is referred to as the Activities of Daily Living as well as the Instrumental Activities of Daily Living. These are medical/health care evaluations more officially done by a medical professional when needed, but a quick evaluation by a geriatric care manager can help guide the big discussion of where is best for long term care needs. While each situation is different and there are many customized personal care plans, there are four main living options:

Option 1—Companion Care: Companion care is when someone comes in to the home to help you continue to live more or less independently but providing assistance only with those activities where help is needed. Companion care can run the gamut from preparing meals, house cleaning, shopping and errands, all the way to assistance with washing and dressing. Companion care can also range from full time to providing a supplement to help from the family. In a lot of cases, this is a first stage of care that may be replaced by a more structured living environment if illness progresses. In many other cases, it is only a temporary measure to assist someone who is convalescing until they regain strength and mobility. In many cases, this is the type of care many veterans, spouses of veterans, or widow(ers) of veterans need financial help with in the form of the Aid and Attendance Pension Benefit.

Option 2—Move in with Family: While this is often a first reaction on the part of a family wanting to help as well as provide some cost savings, there are a lot of unanticipated difficulties. On the part of the person needing help, there are often strong emotional difficulties with having a lot of reliance on family members that they themselves used to take care of. Suddenly, the children that were dressed, fed, and bathed by a parent are now the ones doing the dressing, feeding and bathing, and that can be a tough thing for people to emotionally deal with. On the part of the children, there is often a huge disruption in their own lives and routines for work, school and activities for their kids, and other socializations that had been set for some time.

There is no doubt that this arrangement also has a lot of benefits, not the least of which is that the family is together during a time of difficulty and they can gain much emotional support from each other. And the cost savings compared to some of the other options is also a great benefit to the family. In some cases, moving in with the family has also been combined with the companion care option so that while family members are providing a lot of the needed care, there is someone else coming in to help with some of the activities that the parent would prefer to delegate to a non-family member, or, in some cases, cannot be done by a family member.

In my own grandmother's case, she had moved in with my aunt when it was better that she not live alone anymore, but it reached a point when neither my aunt nor either of her two young sons could lift her from bed to a chair or from a chair to a walker without great difficulty.

Part of the conversation also has to be the potential for "shifting income" in the form of rent or paying family members for help with activities of daily living. Most families are not thinking about being compensated, and in fact are thinking about providing care out of love. But the moving of income from the veteran, spouse of a veteran, or the veteran's widow(er) can be an important consideration when trying to qualify for the Aid and Attendance Pension Benefit.

Option 3—Assisted Living: Assisted living arrangements can range from simply living independently in a more communal environment where prepared meals and dining facilities are available along with organized activities all the way to needing some help with everything short of skilled nursing care. In many cases, assisted living facilities provide the whole range of assistance as needed so there is no need for someone needing more help to move out of the assisted living facility until it is time for more skilled medical care and assistance than the facility can provide.

Assisted living is often less expensive than nursing care, but it is still more expensive than independent living and certainly more expensive than moving in with family. However, there is definitely more that can be done for veterans, spouses of veterans, and widow(er)s of veterans when it comes to assisted living care, but that will be an educational section all on its own.

Option 4—Nursing and Skilled Care: This is often called nursing home care, but the fact is that it really is more accurate to call it "skilled care" because it can be administered in a facility or at home. Many people needing this level of care would prefer to stay at home, and it can be more cost-effective to do so. (When it comes to Care Assistance Planning and having Medicaid or other programs help pay for some of the care, the government is equally willing to have the lower costs of in-home but skilled care since it is cheaper for the government.) In other cases, a facility that provides skilled care may be exactly what it needed, and so staying at home may not medically be the best option for you or the family.

In any event, this is the level of care that often frustrates families the most because, unless they are medical professionals, the care of their loved one is taken largely out of their hands. Again, dealing with the loss of control is difficult for the individual needing care as well as the family, and this is one of the reasons we enlist a geriatric care manager for all of our Care Assistance Planning cases.

While most people come to us to help with the financial aspects of Care Assistance Planning, we have to start with what kind of care is required and preferred by our clients in order to achieve the best possible outcome. After all, saving money is and should be secondary to getting comfortable, competent and appropriate care.

Chapter Three:
Ways to Pay for Long Term Care

"Thank you for meeting with me," Fred said. "I really have no idea what is going on with Mom since Dad used to keep that all to himself."

Fred was meeting me for only the second time, and the first time was nothing more than a quick introduction over the Holidays so Fred would know where to go in case anything happened to his father and his mother was still in assisted living. In the past, I had been meeting with Fred's sister, who was the trustee in charge her parent's assets, and still was. However, she was having trouble explaining everything to Fred, so she asked if I could speak to him.

"I'm afraid I'm pretty lost," Fred said. "The one thing I need to make sure is that Dad didn't somehow mess up Mom's finances. Now that Dad is gone, I told the administrator at the assisted living center that I didn't know what was going on with paying for Mom's care, and they told me that my sister said it would be taken care of. When I called her, she told me to call you."

"It's OK," I said. "Your sister has been working with us for the last few years and she told us it was OK to talk to you. Your father wanted to make sure that your mother's assets were protected, that they would be available for her care, but that once his pension was gone there might not be enough income to cover the costs of care. Since your Dad was a wartime veteran, there is a monthly Aid and Attendance Pension Benefit there for your mother to help pay

for her care, and the paperwork is already in moth with our colleagues at The Senior Veterans Council."

"But I know Mom and Dad had more than a five hundred thousand dollars in accounts a few years ago, they had the house, and a lot of other possessions," he said. "That goes to Mom, doesn't it?"

"Actually, no," I responded. 'The accounts are already in an irrevocable trust under your sister's control to take care of your mother without disqualifying her for the Aid and Attendance Pension Benefit. The house is already in a different irrevocable trust. Your father left nothing directly to your mother, and all of this has been planned for."

Fred looked confused.

"Here," I said, pulling out the copies of the documents and the plan. "Here's what we did."

It's not the job of the Veterans Administration personnel to save your family money. In fact, even if you qualify under the income test (more on that later), part of their job is to advise you to pay for your own care as much as possible until your assets are below a certain level, and only then get you approved for the Aid and Attendance Pension Benefit. So if you simply follow the government's advice in qualifying for this pension, you may end up paying for a lot more than you are legally obligated to.

There are four main ways to pay for long term care, and some are better than others depending on your situation.

Payment Method One: Personal Income

The first method of paying for long term care is simply by paying for it out of your own income. This means diverting some, most, or even all of your income to the care facility in order to cover the costs. The type of care most often needed for senior veterans asking about the Aid and Attendance Pension Benefit is home health care, extra care at a family member's house, or assisted living care. While facility care varies greatly, the average month's stay in an assisted living facility skilled nursing facility in North Carolina is somewhere around $3,000, but can vary from $1,700 to $7,100. For most individuals, this kind of income is not readily available, especially if there is a spouse outside the facility who needs some of the joint income for their monthly living expenses. Nonetheless, income is always considered the first way to handle paying for long term care, even if it does not cover the whole bill each month.

And so people can work their whole lives to earn a pension, reach the age to start social security, and with one bit of bad health it can all disappear. In many cases, even 100% of a person's income is diverted to a long term care assisted living facility to take care of them, it may still not be enough. That leads us to the second method of paying.

Payment Method Two: Liquidate Assets

In many cases, an individual or couple can spend their entire lives working hard, put money away, and then wish to leave the fruits of their labors to their children or other loved ones. Unfortunately, when it comes to expensive long term care, it can drain a lifetime of work in a few years or even months. Selling off stocks. Draining IRAs and 401ks. Cashing in savings bonds and CDs early. When not planned properly, it happens one month at a time all with the hope and prayer that you will get better. And then once you are better and can return home (if you haven't sold that to pay the bills), you may find most of your resources are gone and you have to live on a lot less.

Most of my clients don't like this option, and with good reason. After all, who wants one sickness to take away everything you've worked for and give it to an assisted living facility?

Payment Method Three: Long Term Care Insurance

A third method of paying for long term care is by purchasing long term care insurance, especially in the case of veterans if it pays for home health care at all levels (not just the skilled nursing part). If you are still young and can afford to pay the premiums, then it is worth looking into. In addition to traditional long term care insurance, there are other insurance options that "add on" long term Care Assistance with some more traditional investments. However, it has become almost routine that the people who seek our help with the Aid and Attendance Pension Benefit didn't purchase long term care insurance or did not purchase enough to cover all of the costs. And now that an illness is imminent, they are stuck being either uninsurable or the premiums are much more than they can afford.

A few years ago, a colleague told me about how he met with a client every year about his life insurance and investments, and every year he made the same suggestion. He told his client that if he passed on his wife would be able to continue in her same lifestyle without interruption because of the life insurance on him. However, the reverse wasn't true. If she passed on and he didn't have her pension and social security coming in, he would not be able to retire. Ever. And so he kept suggesting to his client that he get life insurance on his wife only to get laughed off that "there was no way his wife was going to die before him."

Then one day the client walked into his office and said he finally was ready to talk about life insurance for his wife… because she was just diagnosed with stage 3 terminal cancer. Of course, life insurance was now out of the question. It is often worse when it comes to long term care insurance. While everyone realizes they will pass on one day, the thought of not being healthy enough to take care of yourself is almost unthinkable until it happens.

Payment Method Four: Care Assistance and the Aid and Attendance Pension Benefit

There are various programs run through federal, state, and possibly local agencies designed specifically to help people pay for long term care. While this sounds great to many people faced with losing all of their income and assets to a nursing home or assisted living facility (and also finding that long term care insurance is not an option), qualifying for these programs can be very complex. Especially for the Aid and Attendance Pension Benefit if you want to save some of your assets for your family and/or make sure some of your income is available to support a spouse. But as a wartime veteran, spouse, or widow(er) of such a veteran, the Aid and Attendance Pension Benefit is supposed to be there for you if you qualify.

But even that qualification is complicated because we also need to look ahead for the possible need for Medicaid. For Medicaid alone, there are more than 200,000 rules that are changing all the time. That is why it makes sense to work with professionals who both understand the Aid and Attendance Pension Benefit *and* Medicaid Planning. Even if you believe you'll never need Medicaid to pay for nursing level care, you want to make sure you understand how Medicaid could be impacted by strategies used to qualify for the Aid and Attendance Pension Benefit.

It is also important to note that one integral component of Aid and Attendance Pension Benefit planning is possibly (maybe even *probably*) using one of those long term care investment alternatives to make sure that assets are not going to be risked in the market. But it is by no means the only solution. Again, it may only be one of the 200,000 pieces of the puzzle, but we will discuss that piece in more detail later in the book.

There are four main ways to pay for long term medical and assisted living care, but as you've read most people would prefer to save something for themselves for when they get out of a facility or to save for the family when they pass on. There is no need to go completely broke to qualify for the Aid and Attendance Pension Benefit OR Medicaid, but like most things in life it is not always easy to get the help you need without working with the right professionals.

Chapter Four:
The Service Qualification Test

I was sitting with Kevin, a veteran from the Vietnam era, and daughter to discuss the Aid and Attendance Pension Benefit, or as they called it based on their research, the "Aid and Attendance" benefit. Kevin was mentally sharp as a tack, but physically he was starting to need more help just getting by with his daily activities. His daughter Diane were more than willing to help, but he wanted to make sure that he was a little a burden as possible. And so he did a little online research (with the help of his granddaughter) to see if there was a way to afford care. There was. But Diane was skeptical.

"But dad, it says right here that you have to be a combat veteran," Diane said. "You told us you never saw combat."

"Actually, that is not true," I said. "You just have to serve the required number of days when the U.S. was engaged in combat, with active duty in a major branch of service somewhere in the world."

"But Dad never even left the United States," Diane said. "How can he be qualified for a pension for serving during combat if he never left U.S. military bases?"

"Because I served," Kevin said.

"Exactly," I said. "Your stateside service to support the war qualifies. You were there when your country needed you, and you could have been sent into combat at any time. Now, this is one way your country is supposed to be there for you."

There are some simple rules to determine whether or not a person qualifies for the Aid and Attendance Pension Benefit. And I say "person" and not "veteran" because the Aid and Attendance Pension Benefit is open to veterans who served during specific periods of time, the spouses of veterans who served during those same times through the veteran, and widow(er)s of veterans who served during that time period. But there are rules defining spouses and widow(er)s as well.

Service Test for Veterans

The first test is to determine whether the veteran served during the specific dates. If the veteran served before September 7, 1980, the veteran must have served on active duty for at least 90 days, one day of which must have been during war time. That's it. One day was considered war time, and the total time in the service is at least 90 days. But then the question is what dates were considered war time?

For Veterans who have served at some point during World War II through the end of Vietnam, it is extraordinarily hard not to qualify except in cases where service was only between Korea and Vietnam. Here are the dates:

- World War II—December 7, 1941 through December 31, 1946 (please note, this includes the occupation period after the war officially ended).

- Korean Conflict—June 27, 1950 through January 21, 1955
- Vietnam Era—August 5, 1964 through May 7, 1975; (and specifically for veterans who served "in country" before August 5, 1964 it would be February 28, 1961 through May 7, 1975)
- Gulf War—August 2, 1990 through a date to be set by law of Presidential Proclamation. For this war specifically, the time of service is 24 months or completing the term of active duty, whichever comes first.

There may also be other, more complicated rules for veterans serving during other war time periods that it is best to simply say that you should call to find out if the service times qualify. In addition, the pension may be available for service outside of the "traditional" or main branches of military service, such as the Merchant Marines and certain auxiliary organizations.

For Merchant Marines in particular, they were among some of the bravest who served during World War II but were not technically "active duty" with the Navy. They were exposed to the dangers of the German U-Boats serving on ships that were, for the most part, slow and defenseless. If a family member served in the Merchant Marines and can document service on a vessel that traveled the sea lanes that were under attack by German submarines, then they many qualify for the V.A. Pension Benefit. Our colleagues at the Senior Veterans Council can assist in researching the Merchant Marine and Coast Guard records to see if they may qualify.

One thing to keep in mind is that this Aid and Attendance/Aid and Attendance Pension Benefit is only available to veterans 65 or older unless they are completely disabled. In such cases, there are other potential benefits such as Disability Compensation that may be available, but in most cases a choice has to be made between the other compensations and the Aid and Attendance Pension Benefit.

Discharge Status Test

If a Veteran received an Honorable Discharge, then they qualify under this test. If the discharge was "less than honorable," meaning General or Medical, then the circumstances of the discharge will be reviewed by the V.A. Pension Center for eligibility. A Dishonorable Discharge will not qualify for the V.A. Pension Benefit. To find out more about how the discharge status tests apply to your particular situation, please contact The Senior Veterans Council.

Healthy Veteran, Sick Spouses

In some cases, the veteran may be healthy, but it is their spouse who has health issues that are eating up their income with unreimbursed medical expenses. For spouses of veterans, they simply have to be married to a veteran who meets the service and discharge status tests. They also must not have been living "separate and apart" from the veteran at the time, which is a way to say they were going to actually become divorced or were for all intents and purposes divorced even if such divorce was not actually accomplished. In other words, the benefit is actually there to help the *veteran* help *their spouse*, and the pension check will go to the veteran rather than the spouse directly.

Widows and Widowers of Veterans

The qualification of a widow(er) of a qualifying veteran is not as simple as it may seem, mainly because divorces and remarriages matter in this test, but only during certain dates. Here are the specific rules about widows and widowers of qualified veterans:

- The widow or widower must have been married and living with the veteran at the time of the veteran's death.

- If the person had divorced the veteran prior to the veteran's death, then they are not considered a widow or widower for these purposes.

- The widow or widower must not have gotten remarried after the death of the veteran. If a widow or widower remarries, then that widow(er) is no longer eligible for the V.A. Pension Benefit under the Veteran who died. However, if that remarriage ends (for whatever reason) prior to November 1, 1990, then the widow(er) will again be eligible for the V.A. Pension Benefit under the Veteran's marriage. (Note: The November 1, 1990 date does NOT apply to a widow(er)'s DIC Benefit. Regardless of when the remarriage ends, a Widow(er)'s DIC Benefit will be reinstated.)

While the rules seem straightforward, there is no need to simply guess. Sometimes, there are specific exceptions to the rules that only an experienced Accredited V.A. Attorney or Agent would know about. If you have questions about whether or not a veteran meets the service requirement test, simply give us a call at 919-844-7993 and we can discuss it, or contact The Senior Veterans Council through their website at www.SeniorVeteransCouncil.com.

Chapter Five:
The Income Test

I ran into Mom and her daughter Tuesday at the grocery store, which is unusual for us since we usually do the weekly shopping very early on Saturday morning, and the place is pretty empty at that hour. This time Fran and her daughter Doris (not their real names) needed some key ingredients for that afternoon's lunch that they forgot.

"Oh, Mr. Marsocci!" Fran said seeing me. "It's good to see you. I didn't know attorneys shopped for groceries!"

We all laughed at that.

"It's good to see you, too," I said. "How's Don doing?"

"He's doing well," Fran said. "In fact, we're making an apple pie for lunch, and then we'll bring him a few slices this afternoon. It's still his favorite."

"I still can't thank you enough for helping Mom and Dad," Doris said. "Thanks to you, Dad's stay in the assisted living center is still going reasonably well, and Mom still has enough money each month to get by. If it weren't for your help and the Aid and Attendance Pension Benefit, Mom would have been on food stamps and keeping the heat turned off in the winter."

"You're very welcome," I said. "I only helped your Dad qualify for the assistance he deserved because of his service, and I helped your Mom keep all of the income she was entitled to. This wasn't something that was handed out to you. Your Mom and Dad earned it by serving their country when it needed them."

At first glance, the rules surrounding income may seem straightforward, but when it comes to the Aid and Attendance Pension Benefit, it can be extraordinarily complicated. In particular, there are some specific techniques and rules that can be followed which can allow for qualification for the benefit. Because of these tremendous but hidden opportunities, it makes it well worth having qualified professionals generate a complete plan. But for today, we'll look at the income requirements when it comes to both individuals and spouses as well as some of the opportunities to divert income to another family member to help qualify.

Calculating Income for V.A. Purposes

The General Income Test

One of the worst mistakes veterans or their families make is calling the Veterans Administration and asking about the Aid and Attendance Pension Benefit. When asked about the how much income the veteran and/or spouse or widow(er), they usually give out their gross income, or even their net revenue after deductions and taxes. Unfortunately, the reply from the V.A. is usually that they earn too much money.

However, the income number is not their gross income, or even their net income after taxes, but is, in fact, called Income for V.A. Purposes, or IVAP. The first step is determining what counts as income and what doesn't count.

Income that counts for V.A. purposes comes from a variety of sources, including wages, gifts of stock or property received, inheritances received, IRA & 401K withdrawals, Social Security payments received, Social Security Disability payments received, and even gambling winnings. That sounds like a pretty exhaustive list, but there are some big exceptions to what counts as income.

The following sources are NOT counted in the income calculations for V.A. purposes: assistance contributions from non-profits, family assistance program payments related to the upkeep of a veteran's home, life insurance payments or cash surrender value received, Medicaid payments received, V.A. compensation, V.A. DIC, Supplemental Security Income (SSI), other V.A. Pensions such as housebound or other Aid and Attendance payments. In some situations, even installment sales of property are not considered counted income. In addition, any "bartered services" are not counted as income, even though such bartered services are often considered income taxable on 1040 tax returns.

As you can see, just adding up income is not as easy as it first appears. But what about deductions?

Deducted Unreimbursed Medical Expenses

Next, we need to calculate all care expenses not paid for through other sources, known as "unreimbursed medical expense," or UMEs. This includes a wide array of costs related to prescriptions and non-covered medical procedures and health care worker assistance costs.

But in addition to what people consider traditional medical expenses, UMEs also covers a wide array of other non-medical costs, which can include the entire cost of assisted living care… even room and board if specific conditions are met. There are also far too many other deductible costs to list here, especially since there are some very fine distinctions in what can be deducted and what can't that sound very similar.

Income for V.A. Purposes

Once you add all income and then subtract all UMEs, you end up with the actual income for V.A. purposes number. The true IVAP is what the Veterans Administration needs in order to determine whether or not the income test is met, and then also it is used to calculate how much the monthly pension amount would be.

A Technique to Lower the IVAP

In addition to the IVAP calculations making a lot more veterans, their spouses, and widow(er)s eligible when compared to straight "income," there are also ways to lower the IVAP if necessary.

One of the biggest catch 22s that senior veterans go through is tightening the budget too much because they can't afford to hire people to help with care… which means that they have too much in income because the expenses they should have are not offsetting the income in the IVAP calculations. And it is a natural reaction when a person or family is faced with income not being able to cover expenses and the desire to preserve what assets they do have. So what do they do?

They cut back on expenses, especially regarding care. It takes strong, self-reliant people to work in the military, and those characteristics carry through long after service has ended. So veterans and their family members tend to "push through it" and uncomfortably strain doing ordinary activities of daily living.

Unfortunately, this cutting back might be one of the worst things to do. By actually hiring people, sometimes even hiring family members using properly drafted and executed care contracts, the Unreimbursed Medical Expenses can be raised, therefore lowering the IVAP. So where is the money paying for these "extra" but necessary expenses going? Exactly where they should if home health workers or an assisted living facility is being paid to provide the necessary care. Or, even better, family members who are legitimately providing needed service for the veteran, spouse, or widow(er) are getting paid. So the money is actually "staying in the family." Again, however, it is important to structure the care contract to meet both IRS and Medicaid standards.

There are many more small factors in calculating income for V.A. purposes, and veterans and their families want to make sure they are qualified under the income test before spending a lot of time trying to work through the rest of the V.A. Pension Benefit process. If you want to speak to someone to discuss the income test, then please contact us at 919-844-7993, or we can also recommend that you contact The Senior Veterans Council through their website at www.SeniorVeteransCouncil.com.

Chapter Six: The Asset Test

I meet with people all of the time who have loved ones who will need extra care, but, like deer caught in headlights, they are too uncertain to make any move at all, especially when they don't have the right help. As months go by, senior veterans and their families may be losing out on the Aid and Attendance Pension Benefit because they don't know enough to make the right steps, so they take no steps at all.

So what do they do? In many cases, the family steps in and provides actual care without compensation. In other cases, the family provides care by paying for it out of their pocket. In still other cases, the veteran may actually go without the care they need. When there is help from the Veterans Administration, all of these scenarios should be considered unacceptable.

And it is just as unacceptable that a veteran having "too much" in assets is now being forced to spend down their life savings to qualify for the same exact benefit that other veterans will receive. Fortunately, the "too much" in assets problem may be relatively easy to solve.

<u>How Much is Too Much?</u>

In our office, we handle a lot of Medicaid Planning, and the numbers can be a little harsh but they are exact. An individual seeking nursing home Medicaid can keep their own liquid accounts totaling less than $2,000. This can be comprised of checking accounts, savings accounts, mutual funds, and a variety of other investments. But there is that firm number of less than $2,000.

And what about the spouse? How much can a spouse keep? Well, it varies from state to state, but it also is an exact number. For North Carolina at the time of this printing, the amount of liquid "countable" assets a spouse can keep and still qualify for Medicaid is $119,220. But each state has its own number.

But what about the Aid and Attendance Pension Benefit? How much can be kept? The way it used to be was somewhere between $40,000 and $80,000, but some recent changes made the number more exact: $123,600. The old rules left the amount of assets nebulous, forcing Veterans who didn't have professional help to just take their "best guess" in qualifying. But these new rules providing a higher, exact amount came with a tradeoff we'll discuss in a bit.

And now a word about the house. As long as the veteran or the spouse or widower is occupying the house, there is no problem. However, there have been multiple cases of the house being left empty because the care needs were great enough that assisted living was required, and when the V.A. bureaucracy finds out, it may cut off the Aid and Attendance Pension Benefit, justifiably or not, because the house is now in a case worker's eye an available asset. Fortunately, preventing these misunderstandings is handled in the section below.

Asset Transfers

When it comes to Medicaid, there is a "five year look back period" on all gifts. This means that Medicaid will impose periods of ineligibility for nursing level Medicaid for a specific period of time based on the total value of gifts from the five years prior to applying. In this sense, the "gift" is counted as a transfer of assets to anyone, usually a close family member but it still counts as a gift if the money is placed in a trust.

One of the great things about the Aid and Attendance Pension Benefit that was changed with the new rules in October of 2018 was there used to be no lookback period. However, now the rules do impose a lookback period of *three* years, not five.

"Fantastic!" I often hear. "I'll go out and give my assets away today, and in three years I'll qualify!"

Hold on a minute, though. There are a lot of considerations to think about first, and often the best, safest way to handle the transfers is to put the assets in irrevocable trusts like we describe in the chapter on comprehensive solutions.

But in the meantime, here are some reasons why we generally recommend transferring assets into one or more irrevocable trusts rather than giving the money to a friend or family member directly:

- Car Accidents and Lawsuits: Once your money is transferred to your children or other family members, it belongs to them. If they are sued, then your assets could be lost in that lawsuit. If the assets are transferred into an irrevocable trust, then they are protected from lawsuits against the children/family members.

- Inheritance Contingencies. Often our veteran clients trust their child or children enough to transfer assets to them, but what happens if that child passes on? Most of my clients want their assets to go to their children or chosen beneficiaries after they are gone. But if their child dies before you, will the money eventually go to your child's children upon your death? Or will it go to your child's spouse?

- Death of a Child/Family Member: What if the assets do go to your child's spouse. Will their spouse continue to hold the money and use it for your supplemental care and other needs? Or will they have their own needs and expenses? What if your child's spouse gets remarried? Will their new spouse be OK with that money being spent on you? I have been in the awkward position of having to tell the widows and widowers of a child who passed on that they have no legal obligation to continue to use their mother-in-law's or father-in-law's gifted money for their care… and I've had to tell them this in front of the other children.

- A "Stepped-Up" Tax Basis for Real Estate: We'll get more into a specific example in the next chapter, but with regard to real estate, one of the worst things to do tax-wise can be gifting real estate to a child or children. When they receive the real estate as a gift, then they also get the giver's tax basis, meaning if the house were purchased for $20,000 forty years ago but is worth $300,000 when the giver eventually passes on, then the capital gains taxes when the children would be the applicable rate for the $280,000 gain between purchase and sale. On the other hand, with the specifically drafted irrevocable property trust holding the property, then the capital gains taxes will only be the gain or loss from the fair market value on the giver's date of death to the date of sale, and not from the date of the original purchase. Again, a more specific example will be in the next section.

- Income Taxes on Retirement Accounts. Another major factor to consider is that while retirement accounts can be drained and the assets transferred, there are income tax consequences to doing so. That is why income taxes from tax-deferred accounts is often a major topic of discussion when reviewing assets for the Aid and Attendance Pension Benefit.

Because there is currently a three year lookback period, careful consideration needs to be made before making any transfers to family members, and what are the best actions to take if it is time to make those transfers. The next chapter will review the various trusts and related documents in more detail.

Chapter Seven:
Comprehensive Solutions

"But my sister Dawn and her husband went through this with his father, and they lost everything," Ben was telling me. "The V.A. made them spend everything down to less than $30,000 before having the benefit start, and he was in a facility for three years before the pension kicked in. I just don't see how we're going to save anything for my father that can eventually be passed down to me and my sister, and it is a considerable amount of money he earned over his lifetime."

"I understand, Ben," I said. "But Dawn and Charlie didn't come to me or anyone else for help, and then they just spent the money on the assisted living facility under the old V.A. rules. Between what Charlie's dad had in income and the assets he spent down, it was more than three years before he qualified for the Aid and Attendance Pension Benefit. However, we probably could have had him qualified within a few months with the right moves. But the fact is that you came to us now, and we can do much, much more than Dawn and Charlie could do for Charlie's father."

"I've read your materials, and what you're saying makes perfect sense," Ben said. "I just wish that Dawn had come to you before Charlie's father had spent so much. But how come every senior veteran doesn't do this, then? It seems like a slam dunk."

"Not too many people know about the pension benefit," I told Ben. "And often what they do hear isn't necessarily 100% accurate. Fortunately, you and Dawn are getting things done for your father with enough time to qualify pretty quickly based on the numbers we ran. We're getting started now."

"Then where do we start?" Ben asked.

I answered, "First, we set up the toolbox…"

There is a series of trusts, powers of attorney, and other legal and financial tools that should be set up when putting together a Care Assistance Plan for the Aid and Attendance Pension Benefit for a veteran, their spouse, or a widow(er), whether it contains additional protection for Medicaid down the road or not. The important thing is to make sure that the correct legal document plan is integrated with the needs of the pension applicant's assets.

My office usually sets up the whole range of tools just to be sure. Some of the trusts and some of the documents may never be used, but it is far better to have a tool and not need it than to need it and not have it. And when we are talking about debilitating diseases, once the need arises, which may be years after qualification for the pension, it may be too late for someone to sign those documents to cover Medicaid.

I've had family members that waited too long and didn't take my advice in putting together the right legal documents, and because of that he wasn't competent to sign a power of attorney and had to instead be declared incompetent and have a guardian assigned. It was much more expensive, the planning options were much more limited, and because of the three years of procrastination the family lost out.

Here is a brief overview of the standard tools we put together for our Care Assistance Planning clients, first for the mandatory documents in a V.A. Pension Benefit Planning case and then some additional documents we sometimes use for further Medicaid Planning:

Irrevocable Family Trust: The Irrevocable Family Trust is designed to be the keystone of the Care Assistance Plan, holding most of the assets to be protected and containing the actual estate planning instructions for after death. This is where most assets are placed to get the three year clock going for passing of the asset test for the Aid and Attendance Pension Benefit, and it also gets the five year clock going so after the five years has run, all of the assets in the Irrevocable Family Trust will also be exempt from a Medicaid spend down. It is also these assets that will probably be converted in whole or in part to provide some long term investment benefits described below. There is usually one trust for an individual or a couple.

Irrevocable Real Estate Trust: While most of the "liquid" assets go into the Irrevocable Family Trust, there are some specific tax reasons to place real estate into the Irrevocable Real Estate Trust. The provisions of the Irrevocable Real Estate Trust are only slightly different than the Irrevocable Family Trust, but those differences can provide a world of tax difference for your loved ones after death if they sell the real estate.

Without getting too much into the hows and whys, when someone controls real estate when they pass on and their heirs sell it, there are usually no federal capital gains taxes because the property gets something called a "stepped up basis." If the person instead had gifted the real estate to their children a few years or even days before death, then the real estate would not get a stepped up basis and there would be capital gains taxes. For example, if Fred passed on and his heirs inherited a house that Fred bought decades ago for $100,000 and the heirs sold it a few weeks later for $400,000, there would be no capital gains taxes because federal law would have set the "tax basis" for the real estate to be fair market value on the date of Fred's death. If Fred instead had signed over the same real estate to his son Doug the day before he died and Doug then sold it for $400,000, at the 15% capital gains tax rate Doug would have to pay $45,000 in capital gains taxes.

In short, the person or couple planning gets to keep the right to any income generated from the property and keeps the right to live on the property. Even though it is in an irrevocable trust, those rights are enough to avoid losing the stepped up basis for the heirs upon death, but it is not enough that Medicaid can say they still own the property and it has to be spent down. There is usually one trust for an individual or a couple.

Durable General Power of Attorney: The Durable General Power of Attorney can be an extremely useful document during a time of medical crisis. The power of attorney can help someone take control of an ill person's non-trust assets during incapacity. During incapacity, a durable general power of attorney may become critical to reaching the money in accounts kept outside of the trusts to pay for medical or other expenses, dealing with government agencies, signing tax returns, and other legal and financial matters.

One of the saddest things we see in our office is when people we advised years ago to put in place a good Care Assistance Plan come back to us after failing to plan and asking us to at least do a Durable General Power of Attorney so the family can legally transact business and take care of their loved one. But at that point the person is no longer competent to sign legal paperwork so the family needs to go to court, have their loved one declared incompetent, and then report to the court on a regular basis how they have spent money and managed assets. Since a power of attorney is an individual document, there is always one per person.

Health Care Power of Attorney: One of the most common horror stories for married couples revolves around one spouse dying, the survivor falling ill, and multiple children with conflicting views bickering while the doctors and hospital wait for orders to help the dying parent. If the parent had a healthcare power of attorney, they could have assigned one child, or someone completely different, to make their medical decisions if they are not able to. The situation is worse for unmarried couples where family members may swoop in and take control of healthcare decisions, kicking out the partner and not even letting them see their loved one.

Having a healthcare power of attorney allows a person to assign the people they want, in succession, to make these important health care decisions when he or she is no longer able to make those decisions on their own. It is also common for healthcare power of attorney documents to incorporate language regarding the agent making end of life decisions, such as keeping or withdrawing life support or artificial nutrition and hydration. However, most of my clients prefer to make those critical decisions themselves ahead of time in a Living Will (see below).

Living Will: This document is highly dependent on State law, and conditions can vary greatly. For my home state of North Carolina, this document will express your individual orders regarding life support and artificial nutrition and hydration that a doctor should follow, and this is triggered when the person is "terminable and incurable" and/or in a "persistent vegetative state." For the State of New York where I went to law school, the Living Will is nothing more than appointing an individual to make those end of life decisions and not ordering doctors directly.

In the end, the Living Will is your wishes regarding life support and artificial nutrition, whether it is through direct orders to physicians or by naming someone else to step into your shoes and make those decisions on your behalf.

Nomination of Conservator: I often describe this document as a bit of "overkill" in both estate planning and Care Assistance Planning, but it is better to be safe than sorry. Simply put, the Nomination of Conservator is a document naming the people you wish to be in charge of you as a person should a court declare you incompetent and assign you a guardian. So in short, a Nomination of Conservator is a nice way of saying it is a nomination of guardian document for an adult.

Last Will and Testament: While nearly all assets in a good Care Assistance Plan will end up avoiding the probate process because the assets are held in a trust, we invariably find *something* that needs a Last Will and Testament to spell out where probate assets go at the end of the process. But the Last Will and Testament has to be specifically geared to work with the rest of the Care Assistance Plan.

The main reasons this Will has to be different from the normal, run of the mill Will are 1) the only beneficiary of the Will is one of the other trusts, and 2) for married couples *in Medicaid Planning cases* there has to be special provisions to avoid Medicaid coming back and claiming some, or possibly all, probate assets to pay for the care of the other spouse. In many cases, the Will is only a small part of the overall plan, but who wants to lose a few thousand dollars because this small part is not quite right?

Other Professional Assistance: While there are trust and legal document solutions, there is also a need for more comprehensive health and related services. One of the reasons we work with The Senior Veterans Council is that they have a registered nurse, a social worker, and a geriatric care manager on their team helping create a more complete plan than just the "money" part involved in the Aid and Attendance Pension Benefit. After all, we are talking about qualifying for more money in order to pay for care. We want to make sure that we have the right type of health care as well as information on all of the other possible programs are identified for you.

The following are some additional documents we sometimes utilize in a toolbox that is also looking ahead specifically for eventual Medicaid qualification but not always used for V.A. Pension Benefit cases:

Irrevocable Miller Special Needs Trust: In my home state of North Carolina and many other states, this trust is actually irrelevant because of those state's *current* Medicaid rules that make a Medicaid recipient's income irrelevant. But just because the income is not really relevant *now* doesn't mean the rules for a particular state won't change *later* and the trust may be sorely needed then.

As discussed before, since most states simply require all of a Medicaid recipient's income go to the nursing home first then the level of income is almost irrelevant unless their income can cover the entire bill. But in those states where there is an income limit, the Miller Trust can be used to receive the income, have it counted as assets instead of income, and then have those assets "spent down" each month by paying the nursing home bill. There is usually one trust per person.

Irrevocable Funeral Trust: This is a very specific trust designed to hold money for a funeral and related expenses for an individual, and the money in this trust is considered to be "spent" even though it may be held as cash or, preferably, life insurance that has not paid out yet. The reason the Medicaid office is OK with this trust is that it is irrevocable, all of the funds spent have to be spent on funeral and related expenses, and anything left over has to go to the Medicaid office to reimburse them for any money paid for the individual receiving care. Because of this, I encourage my clients to make the typical $10,000 transfer, purchase an irrevocable life insurance policy designed for funeral expenses, and no more since anything left over is lost anyway. It is better to put any additional funds into the Irrevocable Family Trust. There is usually one trust per person.

Revocable Living Trust: Usually a revocable living trust is an excellent estate planning tool for avoiding probate but nothing more. In the Care Assistance Planning realm, it has a whole different application depending on the financial situation. Just as with the Miller Trusts, having the Revocable Living Trust may or may not be actually needed in your particular state, but it is better to have it in case the rules change. The use is specifically to maximize the amount that the spouse *not* needing care can keep.

In some states, often referred to as 50-50 states, there is a minimum and maximum amount of liquid assets that a spouse can keep and the other spouse can still qualify for Medicaid, but it is not as simple as moving money from one spouse to the other. For example, if the minimum amount a spouse can keep is $25,000 and the maximum amount is $110,000 and the couple combined has $112,000, then in non-50-50 states, it is as simple as giving the nursing home spouse $2,000 and transferring the remaining $110,000 to the other spouse. In a 50-50 state, the calculations are different. The $112,000 is actually split in half, meaning the maximum the non-nursing home spouse can keep is $56,000 and not the full $110,000.

So is there anything we can do to let the non-nursing home spouse keep more? Sure. There is also a rule that says any assets in a revocable living trust are countable, even if the asset would otherwise be exempt, like a primary residence. So if in the example above we also have a primary residence worth $150,000, then we can put the house into the non-nursing home spouse's trust prior to the snapshot date and then show on the snapshot date that there are $262,000 in countable assets ($112,000 plus $150,000). So now the calculations are $262,000/2 equals $131,000, and the non-nursing home spouse gets to keep the maximum $110,000. As part of the "spend down," we can now transfer the house out of the Revocable Living Trust and to the non-nursing home spouse's individual name, and the house becomes exempt as a primary residence. This one simple maneuver just saved the non-nursing home spouse $54,000. Because we often are not sure which spouse may or may not need care first, there is usually one trust per person.

As you can see, there is a fairly standard Care Assistance Planning toolbox to help a veteran and their family facing care costs, both for qualifying for the V.A.'s Aid and Attendance Pension Benefit as well as a few added documents for Medicaid Planning. However, it is important to note again that not all of the components may be needed when the time comes. Often, the specific V.A. Planning package is enough, but whether or not more is needed should be discussed with the attorney handling the case.

Chapter Eight:
Finding the Right Professional

I sat across from them over charity hotdogs and salad, enjoying the summer evening weather and the fact that the speeches were over. Unfortunately, the couple knew I worked in the Care Assistance field and wanted to chat about how great their life insurance person was.

"Oh, he was fantastic," he said. "Our insurance agent managed to get my mother a whole bunch of money more in income every month, funded a life insurance policy, and actually got a great deal on a mortgage for the house."

"A mortgage for the house?" I asked. "It was your father, a veteran, who went into the assisted living center, right? Why did your mother need a mortgage if she had a lot of income coming in and the house was paid up?"

"Well, you know," she said as if it were the most obvious thing in the world. "To get more money out of the house to get a bigger life insurance policy. When my mother-in-law passes on, it will leave the family with a lot more money."

"What about your mother-in-law?" I asked. "How much did she get to keep in investments?"

"Well, not much," he said. "She has to keep her checking account below $2,000, right?"

"You mean, your father and mother have to keep their accounts below about $120,000," I said. "Wasn't that made clear when applying to the V.A. for the Aid and Attendance Pension?"

"Oh, no," he said, looking at his wife. "We didn't need to do the Aid and Attendance Pension Benefit once the reverse mortgage kicked in. That provided the money mom needed. Besides, they earned too much income even before the reverse mortgage started anyway."

Now I saw what was going on. I knew for a fact that his parents didn't earn "too much income" once you factored in the assisted living expenses. Insurance is only one part of an overall plan, but there are some insurance salesmen who only think of their commissions. This one maxed out his commission by having the clients needlessly sell off everything to pay the premium on an annuity, and then went back for more by having the mother pull all of the money out of the house to buy an insurance policy.

"Here," he said, pulling out the insurance agent's card. "You might want to work with him."

"Thanks," I said, taking the card with a smile, thinking I'll now know who to stay far, far away from.

There are many different ways to screen planners to help with the Aid and Attendance Pension Benefit, and there are always personal questions people want to ask relevant to their own situation. One of the most important choices a family can make is to choose a planner who will lead the team of professionals helping them and their loved ones. While questions about your personal situation are always important and should be asked, there are also all of the usual questions about experience and education people ask as if they were interviewing someone for a job.

First, before even getting to the questions to ask a professional, the first qualification you should look at is whether or not the professional is accredited by the Department of Veterans Affairs. I am a V.A. Accredited Attorney, and I frequently work with a V.A. Accredited Claim Agent. For example, I work on a lot of cases with The Senior Veterans Council based in Raleigh, North Carolina, but we both work with veterans across the country, sometimes using a local attorney to assist with documents. I am smart enough to know that I can be the point person on the legal end of planning, but the claims agents at The Senior Veterans Council understand the fine points of planning, preparing and filing the applications for the Aid and Attendance Pension Benefit. Together, we can make sure the client gets everything they need.

As for the three questions, I was once pressed by a colleague to come up with three and only three questions that will show whether or not a professional knows what they are talking about when it comes to Care Assistance Planning in general. After all, the insurance agent in the above story probably helped hundreds of clients and their families. He may have even gone to some top schools. But clearly the only thing he knew about Care Assistance Planning in general and the Aid and Attendance Pension Benefit was how to make money. He didn't know or care about maximizing benefit, flexibility, and quality of life for the family. Until a Planner knows more about your situation, some preliminary questions can help test their ability.

Here are the three questions (along with the frustrating, but correct, answers) to ask when screening a Care Assistance Planner:

Question One: Can you use a revocable living trust to qualify for the Veterans Aid and Attendance Benefit or Medicaid?

Horrible Answer: "Yes, anything you put into a revocable living trust is exempt from a spend down." This is about as wrong as you can get. In the estate planning arena, a revocable living trust is a wonderful tool for avoiding probate, but it does nothing to avoid the assets in the trust from being looked at for Medicaid or other benefit programs. The reason this is so is because the grantor setting up the trust maintains control over the assets. There are also other kinds of trusts that may be very useful in qualifying for Care Assistance programs while retaining assets in them, but those are typically irrevocable trusts where you have to give up control and usually do so five years in advance.

Bad Answer: "No, there is no way to use a revocable living trust in the Aid and Attendance Pension Benefit or Medicaid process." While this is not as bad of an answer as the one above, it does show that the professional does not truly understand all of the tools and rules involved in overall Care Assistance Planning. A revocable living trust can, in fact, be an important tool in Medicaid Planning if not for the Aid and Attendance Pension Benefit, but it is not a cure all, nor is it a forbidden entity. Which leads us to…

Good Answer: "It depends." The reason this is the best answer is that a revocable living trust can be used in conjunction with some of the Medicaid qualification rules to save money for a spouse not going into the nursing home (often called the "community spouse"). Since all assets in a revocable living trust are considered countable assets, the trust can be used to first raise the countable assets as high as they can be for the community spouse before shifting, spending and gifting strategies can get to qualification. Recently we helped a client who worked with another Care Assistance Planner, and using a revocable living trust allowed us to plan out an approximate $120,000 in savings beyond the other professional's plan for the husband whose wife needed skilled nursing care. However, while the revocable living trust is an important tool not to be overlooked in the Medicaid Planning Process, it is not going to help qualify for the Aid and Attendance Benefit.

Question Two: Shouldn't I just gift assets right away to qualify for the Veterans Aid and Attendance Benefit or Medicaid?

Horrible Answer: "Yes, absolutely. If you gift everything away today, then tomorrow you can apply for Medicaid or the V.A. pension benefit and qualify." As you've already read previously, this can be one of the worst things you can do resulting in sometimes even more than five years of ineligibility for Medicaid. While simply giving assets away with three years time is a tool that can be used to qualify for the Aid and Attendance Pension Benefit, it is like using a smart phone to hammer in a nail. In the end, it will cause a lot more problems for you than it needs to.

Bad Answer: "Absolutely not! Unless you have five years, you should never make any gifts." While not as bad as the horrible answer, it cuts off what can be an important tool in the overall Care Assistance Planning process when it comes to Medicaid. Simply throwing out that tool altogether is also not a good idea.

Good Answer: "It depends." If there are five years… or even less but still a good amount of time… gifting can be a good part of an overall Medicaid strategy. And in the context of proper planning for the Aid and Attendance Pension Benefit, the act of gifting is actually done to the proper trusts three years in advance… not directly to family members.

Question Three: Shouldn't I just buy long term care insurance instead of trying for the Aid and Attendance Benefit?

Horrible Answer: "No, Long Term Care insurance is just an expensive scam. It's like throwing money down a hole." Long term care insurance… more specifically, the right long term care insurance for the right period of time… can be an extremely beneficial tool as part of an overall Care Assistance Plan if you can get in inexpensively enough. However, with the Aid and Attendance Pension Benefit, we are talking about money that can be used right away to help pay for care. Plus, the usual first step in helping senior veterans who need help is classified more as *assisted living* care, not nursing home care, and long term care insurance is often highly focused just on the nursing level of care.

Second Horrible Answer: "Yes, absolutely. Get the best, longest-lasting and highest payout long term care policy you can." Again, Long term care insurance… more specifically, the right long term care insurance for the right period of time… can be an extremely beneficial tool as part of an overall Care Assistance Plan for the nursing level of care. Yes, that was pretty much the same sentiment as above, because it is just as true that never looking at Long Term Care Insurance is just as bad an answer as always having a massive long term care insurance policy.

Good Answer: "It depends." Again, the non-definitive answer is the best. Buying long term care insurance may be good decision depending on the situation overall, and from there finding the right policy paying the right amount over the optimal period of time for your situation is critical. Even more, as time goes on, the policy may be amended and even decreased to fit changing needs. But in most cases, buying long term care insurance will often not help effectively if there are current or upcoming needs for a senior veteran, whereas the Aid and Attendance Pension Benefit can help those who qualify very quickly if the planning is done correctly.

As maddening as it is to some of my clients and their families, the best answer to all of these questions is "it depends." It's not very definitive, but it is the most accurate when the planner you are looking for is still in the interviewing phase. Until they have all of the information in front of them and have the ability to discuss things with the clients in more detail, there is no way to give a definitive yes or no answer to any of these questions. If a professional at this stage is giving simplistic answers, you know you probably need to keep looking.

Another factor to look at is the experience and accreditations of the professionals you are working with. While State Bars may accredit certain attorneys as "Elder Care Attorneys," that is actually a pretty wide field covering not just Medicaid qualification but general estate planning, social security issues, lawsuits against nursing homes involved in elder abuse, and many other items. It might be a good place to start, but be sure to look further.

Now if planning for the Aid and Attendance Pension Benefit in conjunction with eventual Medicaid qualification in mind is what you are looking for, then there are actually Certified Medicaid Planners™ who are granted that accreditation by the CMP Governing Board based on experience, testing, and good moral character, but this designation is actually open to attorneys, social workers, financial and insurance professionals, and accountants as well. More importantly, it is a more focused designation than being involved in "Elder Law," which may even mean the attorney with a large practice suing nursing homes doesn't even handle Medicaid planning at all. So if you can find a V.A. Accredited Claim Agent or V.A. Accredited Attorney who is also a Certified Medicaid Planner™, then you are starting in the right place. For more information on Certified Medicaid Planners™, please visit the CMP Governing Board website at www.cmpboard.org.

Summary

The Care Assistance Planning process around the Aid and Attendance Pension Benefit is never as easy as it first seems, and the biggest threat to a family's finances may be trying to do it yourself or getting involved with the wrong professional. But working with the right professionals early enough can prevent a potential financial catastrophe for the family.

Chapter Nine:
Financial and Investment Options

It's strange how selective memory can be. It was only about four years ago that I was sitting in the conference room with everyone who was here today, plus their father. The three kids were in such harmony that day. Of course, their father was the glue holding the family together. Stan was the oldest son, and he was put in charge of his father Mark's trusts. The appropriate assets were moved so that Mark qualified for the Aid and Attendance Pension Benefit (under the old rules), but then Stan was left in charge of the investments.

Back then, Mark's investments were put largely into stocks. I recommended making sure that the money was invested safely and securely, even if it meant staying out of the stock market and investing in things like annuities or even life insurance. But Mark's broker convinced Stan to keep the money invested in stocks. "He told me that the market always does better in the long run," Stan said.

"You get that, don't you?" he asked his siblings.

"Oh, yes," his brother said.

"Of course," his sister said.

And now here we were four years later, with Mark having passed on only a month before.

"You lost more than a third of dad's money!" Stan's brother yelled at him.

"How could you be so reckless!" his sister shouted. "There were plenty of other safe ways to invest!"

You see, this meeting was going on in 2010, and the investments that Stan's broker had the money invested in had not come back from the 2008 crash yet. It didn't matter that in 2006 everyone was in agreement that Stan could keep the money invested in stocks. All they were focused on now was that 'Stan lost a lot of Dad's money, which means we lose out.' Yes, memory was a very selective thing, indeed.

In putting together a plan to qualify for the V.A.'s Aid and Attendance Pension Benefit, the family is often focused on making sure that the veteran, spouse, or widow(er) is properly cared for. It often involves changes from how they were living life before. However, once the assets have been transferred into the Family Irrevocable Trust, changes that should also be made may not even be thought of.

So what are some of the investment factors and considerations we have seen over the years?

- Risk Should Be Eliminated: In most of the cases, our client's children and family members may be OK putting their own investments at risk from market losses, but they absolutely, positively do not want to risk losing any of Mom or Dad's money. In general, many seniors are usually becoming more and more conservative in their investing anyway. When we are doing irrevocable trust planning, though, the investments are turned over (at least legally and technically) to the trustee, so the trustee takes it even a step further to look into no-risk or extremely low-risk investments.

- Risk of losing money in the market and Medicaid's response. If V.A. gifts have to be reversed to qualify for Medicaid down the road, Medicaid doesn't care that the stocks were killed in the market for the past 2 years. All they care about is the value of the gift at the time it was made in a traditional or modified half-a-loaf plan, not what the value of the stocks are now. Will you be able to personally serve as your parent's banker and make up the $150,000 in market losses?

- Return on Investments Better than Bank CDs: While there is a strong desire to go with no-risk or low-risk investments, trustees generally want something a little better than bank CD rates or money market accounts. While market returns can swing from 25% gains to 40% losses in a given year, CD rates are (at the time of this printing) around 1%, a little more or a little less. Something in between is often desired, even if the risk of earning nothing is a possibility weighed against the possibility of earning 4-8%, just so long as the investment doesn't actually *lose* money.

- Liquidity of Some Investments: Even with the desire to have some earnings greater than CD rates, the overall investment plan also has to take into consideration some amount of liquidity should money be needed for the veteran, spouse, or widow(er). This is also a factor in determining how to invest the irrevocable trust assets.

So what are some of the investment alternatives, and what are some of the more common compositions of assets?

Permanent Life Insurance: Because there are so many different types of insurance with so many different features, I will simply call this type of life insurance permanent life insurance. The type of insurance typically purchased is with a single lump sum premium. This will allow the life insurance to policy to be issued immediately, provide a larger payout upon death, but also provide the flexibility to borrow against the life insurance at comparatively low rates. This way, if money is needed for the care of the veteran, spouse, or widow(er), then the trustee can "borrow out" the money.

While there are typically many other "living benefits" available, the selection of these should be fairly limited because the policy would be owned by the irrevocable trust. Nonetheless, the concept of life insurance as an investment within the Irrevocable Family Trust remains a strong option for many of my clients.

Fixed, Indexed, or Combination Annuities: Another potential investment within the Family Irrevocable Trust are different types of "non-variable" annuities. An annuity is nothing more than a type of life insurance that requires a lump sum payment, has specific growth provisions, and can be turned into a stream of income by the policy owner. Very rarely is the income stream activated in this context because it is usually a growing asset that the trustee and eventual beneficiaries are interested in. Again, what the trustee is really looking for is something that will provide more growth or growth potential than bank CDs, but they also want to guarantee that the asset will not lose money. Because all "non-variable" annuities are kept out of the stock market and come with principal guarantees, they remain a solid investment choice. So what are the different kinds of annuities?

- *Fixed*: These annuities will provide a fixed rate of growth over a specified period of time. Typically the longer the length of commitment to the annuity, the higher the growth percentage.

- *Indexed*: While the money is not invested in the market, the annuity gains are tied to specific investment indices, often the S&P 500. When the S&P goes up during a specific period of time, the value of the annuity goes up (to a point). When the S&P goes down during a specific period of time, the investment simply remains where it was at the start of the time period. Often this leads to a much better *chance* of the annuity earning more money than a fixed annuity, but the chances of that growth exceeding the fixed annuity increase with the time commitment in the annuity.

- *Combination*: A very popular type of annuity offered by a few different companies is what we are calling a "combination" annuity. Essentially it is four different types of investments wrapped into one annuity. One part is fixed, and the second part is indexed, just like the fixed and indexed annuities. The third part is tied to real estate investment trusts, which in some cases can yield even better returns than stocks. Of course, there are some limitations on the growth of the real estate portion as the trade-off for guaranteeing there would be no losses. And the fourth part is tied to the gold market. It is typical that the value of gold rises when the stock market falls, so it the gold market investments are often considered a "hedge" against the drop in the markets. In other words, if the economy is going well, chances are the indexed and real estate as well as the fixed portions of the annuity are going up and gold tends to remain flat. However, if the economy is doing poorly, then the fixed is still going up, the indexed and real estate portions tend to be flat, but gold may rise. The other great feature of this combination annuity is that the four different investments can be apportioned in whatever percentages you want. While many balance everything at 25% each, some clients wish to have more in the fixed portion and less in the others. Still other clients may wish to leave out the gold or real estate portions entirely. It all depends on what is desired. But the important thing is that in all cases the annuity is guaranteed by the insurance company not to lose value.

Permanent Burial Life Insurance: Designed to be used inside the Irrevocable Funeral Trust, permanent burial insurance can help with the Medicaid spend down process and not "miss" that there will be final expenses. I have heard far too many cases of a person spending all of their savings on nursing home care before qualifying for Medicaid only to be broke when they pass on and have their kids foot the bill. Had the money been properly applied to handle funeral costs during the spend down process, the family wouldn't have been paying for those costs out of pocket down the road.

It is also important to not just buy the insurance but to set it up correctly within the trust so the death benefit pays to the trust and your chosen people can use the funds to provide the right type of service. Naming a person as the beneficiary may jeopardize Medicaid qualification, and naming a particular funeral home may tie your families hands should you be moved far away from that funeral home (to be in a facility closer to a child out of state).

Composition of Assets

One of the most important investment strategies to keep in mind is that there must be some liquidity built into the plan. This is why while many of our clients like the safe investment alternatives provided by annuities, there is limited liquidity in those annuities. At least not without incurring penalties for early withdrawal. But most annuities do build in a feature that up to ten percent of the annuity can be withdrawn each year without any penalties, so that is something. But what if money is needed in that first year?

Here is how we usually apportion about $500,000 in Irrevocable Family Trust assets with the veteran and/or their spouse has about $110,000 to $120,000 on their own.

- The veteran and/or spouse would keep the $110,000 to $120,000 in assets, but those would be spent first if a few bigger ticket expenses came up.
- Within the trust, about $400,000 would be put into an annuity or life insurance policy (again, while the combination annuity tends to be popular, it can be invested however the trustee sees fit).
- And also within the trust, about $50,000 is kept liquid in a checking account or money market account.
- The remaining $50,000 is often placed in 6-month bank CDs, but in at least one case it was seen that the money market account actually was earning more than the 6 month CDs, so instead $100,000 was kept in the money market account.

This strategy keeps $160,000 to $170,000 liquid immediately, another $50,000 available with only six months' notice, and then at least $40,000 a year available each year after that. And this is in addition to any income that may be coming in to the veteran and/or spouse or widow(er). Usually with that type of liquidity, we've struck the proper balance a most clients among securing against market losses, having more growth than bank CDs, but still having enough liquidity in case expenses come up.

While there is no end to the investment options within the Family Irrevocable Trust, there are often some very strong guiding principles that children and other family member trustees tend to follow. But, as always, seek the best professional financial advice you wish and invest accordingly.

Chapter Ten:
Some Medicaid Qualification Rules

While the main purpose of this book is to describe some of the rules and techniques surrounding the Aid and Attendance Pension Benefit, it would be shortchanging you not to at least mention some of the rules surrounding the Medicaid Planning process. After all, there is no 5 year lookback period for the Aid and Attendance Pension Benefit, but there is for Medicaid. *The same transfer of assets into the Family Irrevocable Trust is considered a gift for Medicaid purposes, and it starts the five year lookback period.*

So here are some of the main rules surrounding the Medicaid Planning process which have been liberally stolen from another one of my books *The Long Term Care Solution.* Again, these are rules surrounding Medicaid Planning and not planning for the V.A.'s Aid and Attendance Pension Benefit, so the rules may be completely different. For more insight into your specific situation, please contact a professional who is well-versed in both the Pension Benefit and Medicaid Planning.

Countable, Non-Countable, and Exempt Assets

Countable Assets

Countable assets are the most common assets people want to be able to preserve apart from sentimental, personal items. These are generally the liquid assets that people own that can be converted to cash easily. Consequently, these are the types of assets in a Care Assistance Plan that need to be spent down to the appropriate limits, or converted to assets that are exempt or not counted. For example, the following are considered countable assets:

- Cash, checking, savings, money market, and CDs
- Stocks, bonds, mutual funds, brokerage accounts
- IRAs, 401ks, 403bs, SEP IRAs, Keough Plans, and other retirement plans with a balance (as opposed to monthly pension payments that come to you for life; that is considered income and not an asset)
- The cash value of life insurance and annuity balances (meaning the annuity has not been annuitized yet)
- All autos, trucks, boats, machinery, etc. beyond the first automobile
- Real estate beyond what is Exempt or Unavailable
- Any other deposits that can be accessed or refunded if not used, such as retirement community "buy-ins", pre-paid rent, pre-paid utilities, etc.

Basically, if you can access it and easily convert it to cash (or even not so easily in the case of real estate), then it counts towards the limits you are allowed to keep, or you and a spouse are allowed to keep, and any excess must be spent, converted, or gifted appropriately in coordination with a Care Assistance Plan. (NOTE: DO NOT JUST START GIFTING ASSETS. THIS IS ONE REASON PEOPLE GET IN FINANCIAL TROUBLE WITH THE MEDICAID OFFICE).

Non-Countable/Unavailable Assets

In addition to Countable Assets, there are also assets that are Non-Countable, or better known as "Unavailable" Assets. In these instances, they may be assets that would normally be countable but for some reason are not immediately available or easily liquidated. These assets are:

- An inheritance prior to it being distributed to you
- Lawsuit proceeds before the judgment is collected and distributed to you
- Jointly-owned real estate that would cause an undue hardship to the other owner or other real estate with a legal impediment that makes it hard or impossible to sell
- Other property rights that cannot be liquidated, such as a "life estate" (a lifetime right to live on the property without actually owning the property)

The key to the unavailable assets category is that there is no way to actually get cash from the asset now. In other words, you cannot be denied Care Assistance because you are going to get a large inheritance when an estate settles. However, once the estate assets are in your possession, they end up becoming countable (or possibly Exempt) assets. Some of our Care Assistance Planning techniques involve making countable assets get tied up legally to become unavailable.

Exempt Assets

Exempt Assets are the third and most important category when it comes to a Medicaid Planning spend-down, because these are otherwise countable assets that you get to keep. The list is different for individuals versus couples, and so we'll break this into two lists.

For Individuals

- Cash in the amount of $2,000 or less.
- The home with about $525,000 in equity (again, we're not going to use exact numbers because these can change quickly and can vary by state). There are some major restrictions on the home that are beyond the scope of this section and you should discuss it with a professional.
- One Automobile (again, within certain restrictions).
- Personal Property, such as clothing, furniture, electronics, and jewelry (to an extent).

- Funeral account, burial insurance, and burial spaces (within limits, and for the burial spaces, potentially also for immediate family members).

- Life insurance with no cash value (or with the cash value counted as part of the $2,000).

- Certain other assets that are more appropriate for a conversation at our office.

For Married Couples

- Cash in the amount of $2,000 or less for the spouse needing care; cash in the amount of approximately $115,000 or less for the spouse not needing care. [AGAIN, THESE ARE EXEMPTION AMOUNTS FOR MEDICAID PLANNING AND NOT FOR THE V.A. AID AND ATTENDANCE PENSION BENEFIT. PLEASE REVIEW THESE AMOUNTS SEPARATELY.]

- The home with a $525,000 equity value. There are some major restrictions on the home that are beyond the scope of this section and program that we can address at our office.

- One Automobile (again, within certain restrictions).

- Personal Property, such as clothing, furniture, electronics, and jewelry (to an extent).

- Funeral account, burial insurance, and burial spaces (within limits, and for the burial spaces, potentially also for immediate family members).

- Life insurance with no cash value (or with the cash value counted as part of the $2,000).
- Certain other assets that are more appropriate for a conversation at our office.

The "Snapshot" Date

The snapshot date is simply the date that the person entered the nursing home, and therefore is "locked in" to how their assets were arranged at that time. This is one of the reasons why it is so critical to get a good Medicaid Plan in place before someone actually is in the nursing home and facing a giant financial burden. This is particularly true when a couple is involved because it can greatly affect how much in assets and income can be diverted to the spouse. Here's an Example:

Rory needs nursing home care and his wife Amy is trying to rearrange his assets to help. If Rory enters the nursing home on April 1 and Amy starts looking at their assets on April 3, they look like this:

- House worth $500,000
- Rory has IRAs, stocks, and cash worth $100,000
- Rory has income of $2,000 per month
- Amy has IRAs, stocks, and cash worth $50,000
- Amy has income of $700 per month

Based on these facts, Amy gets some help with putting together their finances and eventually qualifying Rory for Medicaid. In the end with a good Care Assistance Plan, Amy gets to keep about $75,000, she gets to keep the house with some repairs and upgrades, gets all burial and funeral expenses pre-arranged and paid for, and managed to get income of $2,500 per month to Amy. The downside is that she had to spend about $20,000 on Rory's care before Medicaid took over, and Amy does not get to have the maximum "Community Spouse Resource Allowance" of about $110,000.

Now let's take a look at the same facts but Amy starts planning a few months before Rory actually has to go into a nursing home. By shifting assets around prior to the snapshot date and using a simple revocable living trust on a temporary basis, the full $110,000 can be kept by Amy on the Snapshot Date, still take all of the same other spend down steps, but now Amy and Rory didn't have to spend down anything on Rory's care and still get all of the other benefits to Amy. In the end, Amy and Rory came out $55,000 ahead simply by planning two months out.

How is this possible? Why is it this way? It's because most states will allow the spouse outside the nursing home, frequently called the "community spouse", to have UP TO about $110,000 of assets, but it is not done by simply transferring the assets to the community spouse. (In some states, they can). It's done by taking the whole of the cash assets, dividing by two, and seeing how much the community spouse and the spouse in the nursing home get to keep. Again, a good but simple technique using a simple revocable living trust in conjunction with timing the snapshot date made a world of difference. Or at least a $55,000 difference.

The Five Year Rule

This is probably one of the most misunderstood rules around. The five year "look back" period refers to how far back Medicaid will look in Care Assistance Planning to see if there were any gifts or transfers that would trigger a period of ineligibility. Let's take a look at what the Five Year Rule does mean before showing what it doesn't mean.

It DOES mean:

- Have the Medicaid office look back five years from the date of application to see if there were any gifts made.

- Imposes a period of ineligibility for all collective gifts made within the five years before the date of application.

- The period of ineligibility is the sum of those gifts divided by the cost figure determined by the Medicaid office to be a "monthly average cost" of skilled nursing home care (currently about $6,000) to come out to a number of months of ineligibility. (See below in the rule on gifting for an example).

- The period of ineligibility begins from the date of application.

It DOES NOT mean:

- That the maximum period of ineligibility is five years; it can be much more.
- That a gift of $6,000 a year ago already expired because the ineligibility month started when the gift was made (it used to be that way, but it is not under current law)

The five year rule can be a little tricky and can profoundly and negatively impact planning. As you saw in the story at the start of this section, not understanding the fine points can lead to much more than five years before Medicaid Care Assistance Planning starts.

Gifting

Gifting can be an important and effective technique in Care Assistance Planning, but it has to be done in absolutely the right way. Even more important to understand, gifting within five years of applying for Medicaid Care Assistance is not necessarily a bad thing. In fact, many "crisis" Care Assistance Plans we develop include a lump sum gift with an accompanying ineligibility period, applying for Medicaid to get the period of ineligibility started, and then having the family take over paying for care during that period of ineligibility because the net gain to the family (along with the other spend down techniques) still has the family come out ahead.

Probably the biggest misconception around gifting is something I already mentioned: the annual amount of gifting excluded from gift taxes is not excluded from Medicaid scrutiny. The $13,000 amount most people have heard about (which jumped to $14,000 January 1, 2013) only relates to federal gift taxes. It has nothing to do with Medicaid. Another piece of that same misconception is that if the gifts are spread out among a lot of different relatives, then the implications are diluted. Again, this relates to the federal gift tax in that you can give $100,000 as 10 gifts of $10,000 each and it is not gift taxable, but there would be gift tax implications if you just gave one $100,000 gift to a person. As far as Medicaid is concerned, there is no difference since it counts up the total gifts given within the last five years regardless of the recipient or recipients (excepting spouses).

Care Assistance Planning can have a huge impact on the family and a spouse staying out of the facility. Unfortunately, doing Care Assistance Planning the wrong way can also have a huge impact on the family if done incorrectly and not for the better.

Chapter Eleven: Avoiding Bad Advice

"But my bank told me I would lose almost three thousand dollars in interest if I cashed out those CDs!" she said. "They told me I was making a big mistake. And my broker told me not to turn my retirement account into an immediate annuity because I don't have to take out that much money to meet my Required Minimum Distributions, so I didn't do it. Why can't I just keep my IRA?"

"But Judy," I tried to explain. "You can't keep your IRA and get the V.A. benefit for your husband because then you have too much in assets but you wouldn't have too much in income with the immediate annuity. And the accumulated interest on the CDs is $3,000, but you're currently spending more than $9,500 a month for in-home care for your husband. With the V.A. Pension Benefit, it looks like you'll be getting about $2,169 a month. You'll make that up in less than two months under the Game Plan."

"Well, I've been with this bank for years, and my broker made us money in the past," Judy said. "This is all just too confusing, so I'm just not going to do anything!"

Unfortunately, this was based on true story under the old V.A. rules. The Game Plan we provided would have immediately qualified her husband for the V.A. Pension Benefit of $2,169 a month. The documents were set for signature, the paperwork and documentation was just about ready to go into the V.A. once Judy took the recommended actions, but after talking with her banker and stock broker, Judy put everything on hold and refused to do anything because they had scared her into inaction. And it gets worse.

This happened in September of 2018 when the new V.A. Pension Benefit rules with a three year lookback period came out effective October 18, 2018. With the new rule change imminent, we contacted all of our clients to get their plans executed before the deadline. But Judy had been frightened enough by her banker and broker that even with this time-critical warning she still did nothing.

The banker and broker potentially cost Judy and her husband $78,084 in lost benefits over three years because they either didn't know what they were doing or they didn't care as long as they kept making money off their money. Last I heard at the time of publishing this edition, Judy was still spending $9,500 a month out of their own assets to personally pay for her husband's care.

While not every case is as extreme as Judy's, there are many financial, banking, tax, and mortgage professionals out there who may excel in their individual fields but have no idea how to handle Medicaid or V.A. Pension Benefit Planning cases, nor do they really want to gather the expertise to do so. And in many cases, there is a short-term financial disincentive, particularly for the financial and banking professionals, to go along with the Game Plan. Telling a stock broker that they will be losing $7,500 a year on commissions (1.5%) on the $500,000 stocks they are managing doesn't go over well if they don't see the long-term benefit to the client and their family.

However, some brokers and bankers do see the big picture, or at least they see enough of the picture to realize it is in the family's best interest to follow through on the VA Pension Benefit and Medicaid Game Plan. In the long run, these brokers often get that money back under their management and more when the kids become clients, adding their own money to what they eventually inherit from their parents.

Here are some of the pieces of bad advice we've had to deal with over the years when other professionals counsel our mutual clients without understanding the full scope of the rules or benefits at stake.

From Banks

- "Don't move the CDs early because you'll lose all of your accumulated interest. Wait six months so you don't lose the $3,000 in interest" even though clients were spending $9,500 for care each month and this cost could be dramatically reduced by the Game Plan.

- "Our bank has trusts. Let's just use one of our trusts" even though the trusts they were offering were revocable and would do nothing to shelter assets from a Medicaid spend down. Often, a month or more is lost to exploring this alternative before someone in the bank's legal department mentions it won't protect against a spenddown.

- "Our bank provides trustee services. Let's look at the bank being the trustee instead of one of your kids." Under the Game Plan, the trustee is effectively the beneficiary of the irrevocable trust in order to let them access funds in a manner that allows them to give assets to themself and then turn around and give money to their parent(s) without jeopardizing the trust funds. Bank trustees will not take on the trustee role if they are considered the discretionary beneficiary, but the bank ends up wasting months of time and the attendant cost to clients before coming to this conclusion.

Bankers are typically well-versed in the accounts they work with on a daily basis, and sometimes even some additional investments. They understand the ins and outs of their accounts, and therefore they are often compelled to advise people against actions that would cause that particular account to lose money. However, the large majority of bankers are not looking at the whole asset picture as it relates to Medicaid and V.A. planning so they may miss the $6,000-$12,000 a month downside.

From Financial Advisors

- "We can make more money in the market," or "the market always outperforms other investments." The client(s) need for sheltered assets to be guaranteed safe because losses in the market can jeopardize funds designated for the care of our client(s) while simultaneously being valued for Medicaid penalties at the full value before the stocks crashed. The investments need to be safe, liquid, and insured for at least the five year lookback period. Unless a financial advisor can guarantee $12,000 earnings per month without any losses, then market performance is not as relevant as the benefits being sought.

- "You don't want to liquidate stocks because of the capital gains taxes." Whenever we produce a Game Plan, we have already examined the issue of capital gains taxes. While no one wants to pay taxes, when we call for liquidating stocks in a Game Plan, it is because on balance our clients and their families would hate paying $6,000 to $12,000 a month much more then the comparatively lower capital gains taxes.

- "You don't want to turn that IRA into an immediate annuity because you'll lose the ability to control how much money you take out each year and how much is taxable." Much of Medicaid and other benefit planning is based on the value of assets in the name of the client(s). Turning tax-qualified accounts into an income stream means that the asset is no longer on the table, we spread the taxes out over time, and we don't have to liquidate the IRA all at once, incur all of the taxes, and then move what's left into irrevocable trusts to shelter it. Again, the taxes have been considered in the overall Game Plan.

There are many types of financial advisors with varied backgrounds and abilities. In fact, there are even some who are versed in long term care insurance. However, all of them are focused on making your money make money while very few understand the complexities of Medicaid and V.A. Planning. As a result, they are often left like mathematicians trying to solve an equation with too many variables and not enough information. As a result, they sometimes simply go with what they know best. Unfortunately, even the best financial advisor can't generate $6,000 to $12,000 a month to pay for long term care expenses without millions of investment dollars to work with.

From Tax Professionals

- "You don't want to turn that IRA into an immediate annuity because you'll lose the ability to control how much money you take out each year." Much of Medicaid, V.A., and other benefit planning is based on the value of assets in the name of the client(s). Turning tax-qualified accounts into an income stream means that the asset is no longer on the table, we spread the taxes out over time, and we don't have to liquidate the IRA, incur all of the taxes, and then move what's left into irrevocable trusts to shelter it. Again, the taxes have been considered in the overall Game Plan, and usually the tax professional isn't looking at the potential $12,000 a month in care costs.

- "You don't want to set up the accounts that way because now your child will have to pay your taxes." Yes, that is often the case that the child acting as the trustee of an irrevocable trust is also the beneficiary of the trust until the parent(s) have both passed on. Account setup recommendations allow the trustee the flexibility to either report income on a 1041 at the trust tax rates OR declare the income on their own 1040 because it would be at a lower rate and they can then take the "extra" tax money out of the trust. In the long run, the family comes out ahead in saved taxes.

- "You don't want to deal with an irrevocable trust. If you set things up that way, then you'll have to do three tax returns instead of just two. Let's keep it simple." Again, an irrevocable trust means a separate tax return, but we're weighing the potential $6,000-$12,000 per month or more in long term care costs against the cost of one additional tax return.

Tax professionals have to deal with tax code complexities that are constantly changing, just like the 200,000 plus Medicaid rules do. However, their goal is to reduce taxes as much as possible for their clients while the goal of a Certified Medicaid Planner is to blend taxes, investments, and care needs and balance them in harmony with the rules.

From Mortgage Professionals

- "You don't want to pay back that mortgage now because your interest rate is so low. In the future, the mortgage rates will only go up." In many cases, even having a mortgage will stifle any attempts to save the house for the family because now it cannot be transferred, deeded, or even partially sold until the mortgage is paid, and then the property can be transferred consistent with the Game Plan.

- "Because your mortgage rate is so low, you're better off not paying off the mortgage and instead investing the money and earning much more interest than the mortgage rate." Unless the investments are going to yield the entire monthly cost of long term care equating to between $6,000 and $12,000 per month without loss or consumption of principle, then protecting the house is the better course of action.

- "If you need extra money for long term care, we can just do a reverse mortgage." Unfortunately, while reverse mortgages may yield some assistance in the short term, we have seen far too many cases where the health situation worsens, the monthly amount needed for long term care skyrockets, and then the house is ultimately lost completely because ALL of the money is drained from it. The Game Plan we have devised can help save the house entirely, but in order to make the moves needed in a typical Game Plan, the mortgage needs to be paid off and not added to.

Mortgage professionals have an extremely difficult job, and they provide much needed capital to families to better their situation. However, mortgages and the tradeoffs the company imposes to lend money are often an impediment to executing the best Game Plan possible. The same is true about reverse mortgages with sometimes even more catastrophic results. All mortgages have their place in a family's financial outlook, but in many cases just not for long term health care planning.

There are many well-meaning professionals out there helping their clients in their own specialized areas. Bankers helping people save and grow money. Financial advisors helping people invest for their dreams. Tax professionals helping people pay as little in taxes as the law allows. And mortgage professionals helping people afford the things they want and need through financing. But all of these professionals should also understand that changed life circumstances also bring necessary changes in a family's savings, investments, taxes, and debt that need to be addressed in a comprehensive manner. In the case of long term care planning involving Medicaid and the V.A. Pension Benefit, these comprehensive changes often involve moves in a Game Plan the professionals do not address on a daily basis.

Summary

There are many different rules surrounding Medicaid, and they are different from the rules surrounding qualification for the Aid and Attendance Pension Benefit for veterans, their spouses, or widow(er)s. However, a good plan to qualify for the Pension Benefit will also take into account the possible need for Medicaid down the road.

As always, if you have questions, you can contact me through my law office at 919-844-7993 or you can reach The Senior Veterans Council through their website at www.SeniorVeteransCouncil.com.

Afternote

Veterans have honorably served their country, and they deserve our thanks as a country. But more than thanks, senior veterans sometimes also need our help. The Aid and Attendance Pension Benefit is just one way to help out the veterans who do need extra help with medical expenses. This book is just one way of introducing you to some basic information on qualifying for this benefit. However, this is not the end of looking for answers but only the beginning. From here, it is important to fight a very natural paralysis, get a little organized with your finances, and reach out to professionals who can help.

For more information, please contact us at 919-844-7993, visit my law firm on the web at www.LivingTrustLawFirm.com, or visit our colleagues at The Senior Veterans Council on the web at www.SeniorVeteransCouncil.com.

Made in the USA
Monee, IL
04 November 2026

67375599R00066